THE LITTLE BOOK OF SUICIDE: 77 reasons to Kill yourself. In verse.

By David Kavanagh

DramBooks

For my late brother Philip

"The thought of suicide is a great source of comfort. With it, a calm passage is to be made across many a bad night." - *Friedrich Nietzsche*

"Nowadays, not even a suicide kills himself in desperation. Before taking the step, he deliberates so long and so carefully that he literally chokes with thought. It is even questionable whether he ought to be called a suicide since it is really thought which takes his life. He does not die with deliberation but from deliberation." - *Soren Kierkegaard*

"If I commit suicide, it will not be to destroy myself but to put myself back together again. Suicide will be, for me, only one means of violently reconquering myself, of brutally invading my being, of anticipating the unpredictable approaches of God. By suicide, I reintroduce my design in nature. I shall for the first time give things the shape of my will." - *Antonin Artaud*

"I have always thought the suicide should bump off at least one swine before taking off for parts unknown." - *Ezra Pound*

"Suicide is a belated acquiescence in the opinion of one's wife's relatives." - *H.L. Mencken*

"If you must commit suicide, always contrive to do it as decorously as possible. The decencies, whether of life or of death, should never be lost sight of." - *George Borrow*

Published by Dram Books
ISBN 9780954856724
Cover: Terry Christien www.cartoonology.com
Back image by Mark Lynch

CONTENTS

PUPPY LOVE

You bought a puppy for yourself.
You thought it would be sweet.
It was meant to be a close
companion,
But all it does is sh*t and eat.

It has a nasty temper.
It snarls when you get near.
So you've let it have its freedom:
Turfed out on its pert ear.

Now you're feeling such a failure.
You wish that you were dead.
You could have loved that puppy
But you'll take your life instead.

You're left with sacks of dog food
And the stains where puppy peed.
You bid this life farewell,
Around your neck - its lead.

1

CASHFLOW CARES

You have no money.
You have no pay.
You're as skint as a polar bear
In the Hudson Bay.

Pennies run away from you.
Pounds take flight.
It's a massive understatement:
Finances are tight.

Pockets are empty.
Bills are coming in.
Life's not worth a candle
So do yourself in.

Your ancestors are calling.
They whisper 'crown' and 'groat'.
Pick up that 10p craft blade
And slit your poor throat.

FORGOTTEN

Nobody loves you.
Nobody cares.
You sit and droop alone
While your glassy eyes stare.

Gone are all the lovers.
Gone are all the friends.
Better cut to the chase, chum.
Just bring it to an end.

Days seem ever longer.
Nights are longer still.
There's no point hanging on now.
Take out the dying pills.

Unscrew the whisky bottle.
Make sure you're really pissed.
And as you sink away, know that
You really won't be missed.

3

GREEN FINGERS

You've hacked and chopped and
pruned once more,
And sown and tended and planted.
You've watered and drained and
mulched as well
But respite is what's wanted.

You're weary from the constant
rigours
Your merciless garden demands.
You're sick of aching back and arms
And dream of ungnarled hands.

Others see just prettiness.
They never see your pain.
You'd like to raze your bloody
garden
And make it bare again !

Take out your old worn secateurs
And press them to your throat.
One last clip through human flesh
Should prove an antidote.

4

LOVELORN

No matter how hard you try,
No matter what you do,
This person you'll forever love
Refuses to love you.

All the sighing lies behind you,
All the aching lies before.
More agony and sorrow
Are heading for your door.

Take out your loved one's picture
And press it to your breast.
Take out your sharpest knife
And do it not in jest.

As the blade cuts through your veins
And the red stuff starts to flow,
Remind yourself that 'Love'
Caused this grim scenario.

COMMUTING

Miles and miles each day you travel
Just to get to work.
The younger you could easily hack it
But now you feel a berk.

Freezing mornings on the train.
Nights spent on the bus.
You'd tell your boss to stick his job
But you're too much of a wuss.

Mortgage payments weigh you down
Yet motivate so well.
And if you want to keep your wife
You'll keep this living hell.

Today the train comes roaring in
And everyone steps back.
You skip forward with a curse
And hop down to the track.

ANCIENT

You feel so aged and ragged.
Your bloom of youth has gone.
There are just saggy buttocks
From whence the sun once shone.

Your dewy skin is wrinkled,
Your fingers crooked and old.
There isn't room for cowardice.
This is the time: be bold.

Take out that rope you've cherished.
Place a stool so you can reach.
Ne'er mind they'll find your body
Like an over-rotted peach.

Farewell to all your troubles.
Goodbye to all your cares.
Old age can't undermine you
When you're swinging from the stairs.

7

SINGLETON

You love your independence
And hate the sight of babies.
You're married to your single life.
It's fun ! No ifs or maybes.

At least that's what you say
When anybody asks.
You 'like to have no partner'.
You quickly wear your mask.

But the mask is wearing heavy
And eating through your face.
You're just too unattractive.
Your acting is misplaced.

You've booked your single cruise
again
On a singles ship.
No-one cares about your tears
So take a fatal dip.

SALAD DAYS

Others are so experienced
While you are just naive.
You'll always lag behind because
You never feel at ease.

Always blushing crimson,
Forever talking timid.
You're barely in your 20s
But guess you've reached your limit.

Expectations weigh upon your head.
Depression mires your soul.
You're better off, you think,
Without this rigmarole.

Climb that daunting crag
With young and sturdy legs.
Bon voyage ! Then launch yourself
Off the crumbling edge.

9

BANKRUPTED

Your business acumen
Has long ago expired.
In debts and unpaid bills
Your fortunes are now mired.

Your cheery bank manager
Is more or less abrupt
Since his favourite businessman
Declared himself bankrupt.

Bailiffs haunt your days.
Court judgments ruin your nights.
You've given up the ghost.
You've run out of all your fight.

Smash your company statuette
And grind up all the glass.
Eat each glistening handful.
End this monetary morass.

10

ADIPOSE ADIEU

Your belly wobbles as you walk.
Your chin jiggles as you chat.
There is no truer explanation.
You're surely just too fat.

Short of breath you climb the steps
And, wheezing, reach the top.
What an awful way to live.
It's better now to stop.

Pile those jammy doughnuts
Into a funeral pyre.
Douse yourself in finest brandy
Ready for the fire.

Only when you've gobbled madly,
And gorged your stomach tight,
Strike a match for better times
Then set yourself alight.

MIRROR, MIRROR

Children rush away from you.
Dogs howl and all take flight.
You cannot get away from it:
You are an awful sight.

Plastic surgeons shake their heads.
Paparazzi guard their lenses.
When you slip outside to walk
You horrify the senses.

Take that mirror off your wall
And smash it hard to bits.
Being ugly's such a drag.
It's only death that fits.

Find the sharpest shard of glass
And press it to your breast.
Two deep stabs should be enough
To lay you to your rest.

BABY BLUES

Children don't bring happiness.
That is what they say.
But you have wanted nothing else
Until this very day.

IVF and acupuncture
Bolstered by your charms
Have still not brought your dearest
wish:
A baby in your arms.

Other mothers sympathise.
They say is doesn't matter.
You smile and go along with this -
A barren wombed Mad Hatter.

Tonight, as they tuck up their
youngsters,
You lie in Baby's empty cot.
You tie its rompers round your
throat
With a very loving knot.

13

SHAMBOLIC

Despite your best intentions
And hopes as you set out,
You've finished up a sham.
Of that there is no doubt.

Ambitions are all thwarted.
Aims have gone awry.
There is but one conclusion:
You may as well die.

Jump in the nearest river.
Down and down you'll go.
(Put weights into your pockets.
It will speed your cheerio.)

No more hopeless striving.
No more useless strain.
And if the river doesn't work
Try a speeding train.

14

SCHOOL'S OUT

Daddy wants you to go in the Army.
Mummy would rather the City.
You'd rather go fishing each day
if you could,
And therein lies your great pity.

You went off to school all alone aged
just six.
You got used to finding your way.
Yet your parents are still directing
your life.
Is it you or those two who hold sway ?

Public school can be harsh and unfair.
It puts your mind in a weird sort of
muddle.
You want to please home with teachers'
reports
But frequently you need a cuddle.

Now the dam of resentment has broken.
The waves of cold anger run deep.
With Daddy's new shotgun caressing
your chin,
You prepare for a longer term sleep.

15

SHORT-LIVED

Your neck is pained from craning it.
You're tired of looking up.
Being short is long on grievances,
Not least God's grand cock-up.

You were not meant to be this way,
Forever staring skyward.
Instead of tall and statesmanlike,
For shortness you're a byword.

Friends and colleagues laugh at you.
You take it on the chin.
They'll never know the bitterness
Or rage that burns within.

Climb that tree and choose a branch.
(You'll need a step and how).
Tie on the rope and stretch your neck.
At least you're taller now.

16

CHAMPION

You still polish your trophies and
medals
From sports triumphs so long ago.
You're middle-aged now and quite
paunchy
But you cannot forget the warm glow.

You became a sporting superstar,
A gilded, glorious youth.
Today you struggle to put on pyjamas.
That's the shameful, inglorious truth.

You could run like the wind and swim
like a fish.
You scored goals like a Beckham or Pele.
Once the proud holder of Victor Ludorum,
Now you strive to hold in your pot belly.

Put out your gleaming silverware.
Burnish it again if you must.
As you swallow acid, remember:
All sporting success turns to dust.

TECHNICAL HITCH

Computers only vex you.
Ipods cause you pain.
You've tried to love technology
But your efforts are in vain.

You'd rather use a pencil
Than a fancy, winking screen.
But all around are dissing you.
It makes you want to scream.

You'll never like this new world,
Created without your nod.
You feel much like a bricklayer
Told to down his hod.

Pick up your PC's cable.
You'll find a novel use.
It will never drive you mad again.
That cable's now a noose.

18

OBSESSED

You wash your hands each hour.
You clean your teeth to order.
Your house is incredibly neat.
You've got Obsessive Compulsive
Disorder.

At one time you were pleased
To be such a perfectionist.
But you've slowly come to realise
These routines are an iron fist.

You're trapped within their grasp
Like a bird in the jaws of a cat.
It's time to make your escape:
Pull a rabbit from the depths
of a hat.

Tonight, at precisely midnight
With the housework perfectly
finished,
You'll brush your teeth with
domestic bleach
And your workload will be neatly
diminished.

19

MUM & DAD

Your parents are knocking on now,
Both in their 90th year.
You wish they'd pop their clogs
But they're full of beans and cheer.

Daddy still does press-ups.
Mother walks the dog.
The Grim Reaper sidles by
Yet declines to go the whole hog.

You're sick of being lectured
And treated like a child.
You're nearly 49 and know
You're far too meek and mild.

You've come to loathe your parents
And yearn for something better.
That's why you're about to strangle
yourself
With last year's Christmas
sweater.

20

STARRING ROLE

Fame has always been your goal,
The glitzy thrill of Hollywood.
But while you primp and preen
like mad,
You're still stuck in Collywood.

No acting course has led you yet
To any sort of casting couch.
With your 50th year now looming near
No wonder you're in a furious grouch.

All that money scrimped and saved
For botox has been wasted.
All the acting lessons you've racked up
For success you've never tasted.

At last the crowds are gathered
And cheer you on, you're certain.
Step off the roof of that furnishings
store.
This is it - your final curtain.

21

CAUGHT OUT

Your reputation has been trashed.
You've been caught with your hand
in the till.
For every person who thought of
you well,
There's a dozen now thinks of
you ill.

Greetings are no longer extended.
Doors are suddenly closed.
When you took those few quid you had
no real idea
Of the calamity it would impose.

Your job has certainly vanished.
Your self-worth is hitting the floor.
Your funds are almost extinguished.
This has shaken you right to
your core.

Dress as you would for an interview.
Wear your finest, bespoke suit and
smart tie.
Take a moment to ponder your folly.
Drink that poison, chin up, and
then die.

GENDER TRAP

You were born a boy but took no joy
In having a penis and balls.
You'd rather be female and sexy
And the fact that you're not rather galls.

In public you swagger and swear like
a man.
In private you dress like a woman.
You just cannot face any op', you
now know
So it's sad coup de grâce that is
summoned.

Dressed in your finest mauve
chiffon,
Your lips crimsoned red through
your tears,
You climb to the top of your bachelors'
block
While vodka helps steady your fears.

As you throw yourself off, you are
minded
To watch your reflection go by.
Your last thought of all as you
plummet to earth
Is: 'I forgot to mascara one eye !'

23

VIRGINS WAVE

You are a Muslim terrorist
And hater of the Jew.
If there's a victim of injustices,
No surprise - it's you.

If you can't kill any Judah
You'll kill a western man.
You'll go out all in glory.
At least that is your plan.

You amble to the checkpoint
And catch the soldier's eye.
Too late he understands at last
He's also going to die.

Somewhere in your mindset
Seventy-two virgins motion.
You're off to sexual paradise.
Clap hands for the explosion.

24

EMPTY NEST

The kids have all departed.
They've left you feeling blue.
Your other half is boring now.
You don't know what to do.

Each day you huddle in their
bedrooms,
Trying to smell their skin.
You feel lost without your 'parent'
hat.
You need your younger kin.

E-mails are few and far between.
Telephone calls are rarer.
You'd travel far to kiss them all.
They say keeping a distance is
fairer.

Sit in little Johnny's chair.
Take tea in Sarah's cot.
Swallow pills in Jamie's bed
Then off to sleep you trot.

25

SPOKESMAN

You're tired of sitting in a wheelchair.
You're always staring up
At endless chins and helping hands
Since your poor legs went kaput.

You're sick of being pitied
And getting sympathetic smiles.
If only your damn limbs would work
You'd surely run a mile.

You try to be so upbeat.
You blink away the tears.
They'll never understand your view.
They'll never get your fears.

You head towards the motorway,
Full of fun and jokes.
'Enough !,' you laugh.'This is the end !
Eat my flattened spokes !'

26

BRIGHT SPARK

Bones protrude from pallid skin.
Eyes are sunk in sockets.
Doctors outline a healthy diet
But you appear to mock it.

They've sent you to an awful place
Where you have to eat your greens.
How could they be so stupid ?
How could they be so mean ?

You try to force a pea down
But it doesn't want to go.
You've never felt so bullied.
You've never felt so low.

There's a lightbulb in the bedroom.
You're certain to eat that.
They'll find you there next morning.
At least you fought the fat.

27

OUT THERE

You sit at your window,
Watching life pass you by.
You never go out.
You don't even try.

You're trapped in your house
Like a modern-day hermit.
You feel like a foreigner
Without the right permit.

You buy all you need
On your computer at night.
But friends have lost patience
And money is tight.

Punch a hole in your window.
Stick a hand in and twist.
There's a very sharp edge there,
Just right for your wrist.

28

DARKNESS

All your life you've lived in the dark
And walked with a dog or a stick.
Now your wife has finally left you
While your pooch is terminally sick.

Once, laughter lit up the shadow
And kisses brightened the night.
You're feeling quite low and
depressed.
You're looking a pitiful sight.

The dog has gone to the vet
And you know he'll never be back.
So you're sat by yourself in the
gloom,
Determined to have one last crack.

You've turned on all the gas taps
And prepared a favourite cigar.
In 10 minutes' time you'll light up
the street
With a blast that will carry you far.

DOWNHILL

You'd love to be a supreme skier,
Whizzing along with all your
friends.
Though you're really not cut out for it,
You despise the message that this
sends.

You've always battled personal
weakness -
Physical feats have quite enlightened
you.
And then it came to downhill skiing -
The very thought of which quite
frightened you.

For years you've stuck to learner
slopes
And let mates' catcalls burn your soul.
You pretended you were happy
Despite the torment and the toll.

Well, today is going to be very different.
You hurl yourself off piste with glee.
You can't hear friends' warning calls.
You're aiming for a killer tree.

HAIR TODAY

You've often regretted leaving school
Without the smallest qualification.
You trained to be a hairdresser,
A role not known for its edification.

While ladies yak about their hair,
You question them about their
holidays.
Your friends have married and live
in style
But your sole comfort is long-gone
glory days.

You were the best kisser in your
school.
(Of that there is no genuine doubt.)
But then you see today's mirrored
image:
Less pussycat doll - more old trout.

Tonight you lock the salon door
Then take a swig of gin.
You wire up some faulty curlers
And plug your fingers in.

31

TEETH TROUBLE

Dentists always smiled at you.
They loved to take your money,
Just to keep your teeth in place.
You never found it funny!

But your gums have still gone
rotten,
And your teeth are falling out.
You've spent a bloody fortune.
For what ? For bloody nowt !

When you bite on something hard
Another tooth will fly.
You can't face wearing dentures.
You'd simply rather die.

Strip the cover from that plug wire.
Prepare with all your might
To use your few remaining teeth
In a fatal bite.

32

PLEASE SIR

At the start you loved your pupils,
Every single one.
Then you realised the truth:
You'd rather they were gone.

Their questions now are tedious,
Their little games a bore.
For 20 years you've laboured on.
You know what lies in store.

More little prats in silly hats.
More yobs and bad behaviour.
You're too tired and old to
retrain now.
Let death be your quiet saviour.

At the end of summer holidays
You're dreading yet more strife.
But your adapted starter pistol
Will loudly end your life.

33

WRITTEN OFF

You're a newspaper columnist.
You're usually in a mood.
Your venom-laced-with-vitriol
Could poison a rattlesnake's food.

You've spent years skewering
idiots -
But fear you're paid too much.
You drown your sorrows regularly.
You know you've lost your touch.

Younger rivals take the piss.
They think you're weak and old.
You revert to philosophy,
Those books now in green mould.

Socrates ended it with hemlock
But you choose a steamy way out:
Three black hookers in your bed
And cocaine up your snout.

MARCHING ON

You're a dignified old soldier
Who glorified his regiment.
But the qualities that made you
Are now merely an impediment.

You'd like to bayonet louts
And machine-gun all the thieves.
But the molly-coddling Law
Has left you rather peeved.

If you grabbed a conman by the throat,
He'd squeal and tell the police.
The tenets of society
Are barely in one piece.

It's time to search the attic
To find which box it's in:
That faithful old grenade.
You pause - then pull the pin.

35

COOKERY LESSON

You've worked in a kitchen
Since you were 16.
The next Gordon Ramsay ?
That was your dream.

But you've failed at French food
And your British is worse.
Your culinary ambitions
Have turned into a curse.

So now you're on sushi
With a Japanese boss.
But he's quite unimpressed
And won't make a loss.

A puffer fish liver
Serves you your fate.
It slips down your throat:
Death on a plate.

36

WEALTH CHECK

There is no God.
Of that you're sure.
You're rich materially
But spiritually poor.

Others draw succour
From something Up There.
It's always eluded you,
The comfort of prayer.

You're sick of the luxury,
The diamonds and gold,
The empty ambitions,
The keep-growing-old.

Tonight at 12.30,
When all are in bed,
You'll eat all your jewellery
To make yourself dead.

FARMED OUT

You've always been a farmer.
You've always worked the land.
Now supermarkets harass you.
This was not what you had
planned.

You're renting out your fields
To any Thomas, Dick or Harry.
Your margins are so small
You have no time to tarry.

All your ancestors were farmers,
Beholden to no-one.
Now you bend the knee and bow
To Tesco/Morrisons.

Today sees your last harvest.
You think it's time to go.
You'll clamber up and jump
Into a shiny grain silo.

DRIVEN MAD

You're a long distance lorry driver.
It's what you've done for years.
It used to pay your bills
Which helped allay your fears.

But the time you spend away
Has quite messed up your life.
Your mate no longer calls
And he's flirting with your wife.

You're exhausted from the effort
Of hauling stuff for miles.
There's very little money in it
And even fewer smiles.

Your sandwiches are off today.
You should have used the fridge.
You jerk the wheel and steer that
truck
Right off the bloody bridge.

39

SHOWBUSINESS

You're an agent for celebrities
But most are minor stars.
They'll only win an Oscar
When Man is found on Mars.

You're petty with the journalists
Who interview your pets.
You like to nag and whine
That it's only you who frets.

Joe Public can go to hell
When you're in the Carlton Club.
Surrounded by your harpy chums,
You raise the level of hubbub.

But your confidence is all a sham.
Your business is in debt.
They'll find you dead tomorrow
Where your weedkiller is kept.

40

MARRIAGE VOWS

Long ago you loved your husband
And enjoyed your wifely duties.
Now he's old and bald and rude
And in love with TV 's auto-cuties.

Where did it all go so very wrong ?
You frequently pause to ask yourself.
Would it really have been so bad
Had you been left upon the shelf ?

You've tried to put the romance back
But it hardly seems the easiest work.
Shame your husband can't renew
himself:
Be born again - a new Young Turk.

Tonight you'll cook a beautiful curry.
You'll light candles and bake fresh
bread.
You'll secrete enough poison to kill
you both
And ensure your marriage is finally
dead.

41

DRUGGED UP

A spliff was all it was at first,
Smoked with some delight.
Cannabis was just so cool.
You never felt uptight.

Then you tried some other stuff
That set your pulse a-racing.
The thrill got better still
Despite your wibbly-wobbly pacing.

Suddenly, all the fun expired
When addiction called your name.
Heroin and crystal meths
Were beasts you could not tame.

At last you start to recognise
Your brain is now unhinged.
You contact all your dealers
And go out on one last binge.

42

JILTED

You had a great relationship.
You felt spoilt from head to toe.
You never saw it coming.
Now you've got the big elbow.

The love of your life
Has left you shocked and bitter.
The church was even booked
But your boyfriend is a quitter.

Frantic messages are not returned.
Then emails go astray.
Your humiliation is complete.
It's the end for your Big Day.

Tonight you write a final note,
Drinking bottle after bottle.
You put on your wedding dress -
And with its train...self-throttle.

43

HOLY ORDERS

Your parents were so proud
That you disdained all earthly
toys.
The priesthood was your calling -
As were the pretty altar boys.

All your knowledge and your skill
Made you a super Catholic.
You looked down on your poor
flock
And considered it quite thick.

For years you lorded it around.
In every trough, your snout.
But your love for altar boys
Has finally caught you out.

As a rabid tabloid newspaper
Now calls you quite unhealthy,
You sink all the vestry wine
And flutter from the belfry.

44

ON THE SIDE

At first it was exciting
When you became your boss's
mistress.
But now you see the drawbacks
Of being just a temptress.

He spends most time at home
With his loyal wife and kids,
While you're left with seedy shags
And a few more extra quid.

You wanted hearts and flowers
But now you're up the spout
He's told you to get rid
And even had a shout.

Tonight you'll send his wife the
details
In a coldly thought-out plot.
Then you'll cut your wrists and join
Your blameless, unborn tot.

45

DRINKIES

It started with the shandy
And teenage alco-treats.
Now you daily take your whisky
But only like it neat.

Vodka is another favourite
And, really, so is gin.
You've lost all sense of balance.
You prefer to pack it in.

You pour your first at 7am
To steady a shaky hand.
But you're tired of feeling guilty
In a hazy borderland.

AA meetings bored you
And you haven't been back since
Your doctor said your liver's f*cked
And you stumbled on absinthe.

46

JOBLESS

You're one of those people
Who just has to work.
You can't sit around.
You feel such a jerk.

But you've been unemployed
For 17 years.
You've become unemployable.
It's all your worst fears.

You've haunted the Job Centre
And job sites online.
There's no need for your skills.
Your trade's in decline.

Tonight you'll open your toolbox,
And do it by rote,
Take out a sharp blade
And cut your glum throat.

47

AIRWAVES

You've always been so talkative
And never sought a mentor.
You found the perfect role
As a radio presenter.

Up each day at 3am
You broadcast to the nation.
But your cheerful voice belies
Your soul's deepening stagnation.

Black depression marks your night
When nobody's around.
In your nightmares, you can't speak.
Your voice cannot be found.

This time when you take a break
You choose a white sand beach.
You swim so far in perfect calm
Until you're out of reach.

48

OPEN WIDE

You wanted to be a healer
But your hopes did not persist
So you settled on the money path
Of being a private dentist.

Mouths are now just cash to you.
You know that is the truth.
Gums are golden earners
And so's a rotten tooth.

But your customers have left you
Since your shameful diagnosis.
You feel a sham to all around -
You're suffering halitosis.

Frenzied efforts to fix yourself
Have only made it worse.
You plunge a needle to your heart
And damn this oral curse.

49

IN THE MIND

You never really shone at sport.
You were better at biology.
The sciences were good to you.
Now you're Professor of
Psychology.

Anything about the mind
Is normally up your street.
You've theorised at dinner parties
With barely time to eat.

No-one ever recognised
That inside you felt sad.
You've always been a bit afraid
You're medically quite mad.

Beethoven playing in the gloom,
You chart your life by graph.
Then you down some sleeping
pills
And take a final bath.

50

SEEDY END

You disappointed your mother,
(A stolid, court stenographer),
By going your own way -
And becoming a squalid, squat
pornographer.

Any man, woman or beast
Was welcome to your parties.
You could have rivalled Caligula
With those exploits in your 40s.

You had seen and done it all
By the time you were 72.
Your magazines have now gone
bust
And your perversions broken
you.

Tightly bound in leather gear,
You determine to go out on a high.
Tracy rams you with a dildo
While Sharon chokes you with a tie.

51

POLITICAL FALL

You slithered along quite nicely,
Taking the road to perdition.
You smiled and oiled the wheels
In your role as a politician.

You never went against your party
Or stood fast on a principled point.
You acted like the sort of MP
Whom only the gods could anoint.

A post in the Cabinet came to you
Just as soon as you expected.
But the voters were not to be
fooled
And now you've failed to be
re-elected.

One last time, you take out your
yacht
Down in your coastal constituency.
You snort cocaine and drill the hull
With a dour, statesmanlike
expediency.

52

WILD AT HEART

You never warmed to office work.
It made you want to hide.
So you chose the perfect job
As an African wildlife guide.

Stalking lion, rhino, and elephant
Put a curious grin on your grateful
face.
Potting game meat for camp
supper
Showed you were in your rightful
place.

But now tourism has all dried up
And no-one pays your bills.
No-one cares about your stalking
Or your super shooting skills.

Tonight you'll down a quart of
whisky
And lie outside your tent.
When the lions come growling by
It's human meat that's rent.

53

BEAUTY ROUTINE

It's not easy being beautiful
With so many eager to inspect
The longer limbs and flawless skin
Belonging to a stick insect.

Forever living on a diet,
Eschewing food and drink.
You're so very tired and listless
You can often hardly think.

Glamour shoots and cover fronts
Are starting to feel a drag.
But now it's far too late to say
That this is not your bag.

Relaxing by the pool again
You stretch out with a book.
No-one sees you down the pills
Which make you come unstuck.

FLYING HIGH

You like to coast at 30,000.
You always know what's what.
From take-off to descending,
You never miss your spot.

But a pilot's day is very long.
You're often deep in thought.
If earthly life is so worthwhile,
Why are you distraught ?

Stewardesses serve more drinks.
Passengers laugh a lot.
None could ever contemplate
Or know your sudden plot.

When your co-pilot goes to chat
You quickly lock the door.
You point the plane towards
the sea
And lie down on the floor.

TRAVAILOGUE

You've travelled all over the world
And written about it in books.
You've muttered smatterings of
Swahili
And earned some funny looks.

On each separate continent
You've left your personal stamp,
Journeying with a practised air
Across tracts dry or damp.

But at home you live a lonely life
And few now come to call.
You're famous for your books
But was it really worth it all ?

Tonight you travel to your corner
shop
And buy some gin and pills.
Then you travel to your attic
Where your mixture quickly kills.

TWEET TWEET

All your life you've studied birds,
From little wrens to eagles.
You've photographed and sketched
them, too,
From harriers to seagulls.

But now your interest has dried up
And you've found you're left alone.
Your family's dead, you have no job,
Your heart has turned to stone.

Your feathered friends stay hungry.
You no longer put out bread.
With nothing left to spark your mind
You wish that you were dead.

Bird mags you've collected,
You heap into a pile.
You sit on top with paraffin
Then light them with a flighty smile.

57

POLEAXED

When you were a little girl
You danced and sang out loud.
You were such a pretty thing.
Your parents were so proud.

When you were a teenager
You were given your first kiss.
The sun shone, the sky was blue.
Nothing was amiss.

Yet you fell in with poor company,
Kissed by every chancer.
By the time you'd reached 23
You'd become a sad pole dancer.

Tonight you'll dance alone
When the club is shut.
But you'll drop hard upon your
skull -
Instead of on your foot.

58

RECESSION

'Mr Money' was your nickname
But it ceased to be a joke
When the markets plummeted
And your cocky bank went broke.

Executive pals crowded round.
You tried to reassure them
That their bonuses were safe
As you could still procure them.

But your confidence has waned.
Your chums have lost their jobs.
Their panic and resentment
Are joined now by their sobs.

Your post is next in line to go -
Your salary won't be paid.
You start your helicopter
And try to eat a rotar blade.

AUTOMATON

Your cars were your beloveds.
You drove them here and there.
Even in a traffic jam,
You loved their pretty purr.

Jaguar and Ferrari
Were your favourite brands.
You also had two Porsches
And your Lotus was just grand.

Yet your lovely cars are rusting
After your motor business fell.
You can't afford to run them now.
It's an automotive hell.

You tie a rope around your neck
And secure it to a tree.
You stamp your Mini's pedal
Then count out:'One, two, thr.. !'

LAWMAN

You became a police officer
To impose all righteous law.
But crooks laugh at the courts
And that's not the only flaw.

Thugs stab whom they like
While prison's a university.
Yet you're on another course
To pander to 'diversity'.

Now you've punched a gay man
Who threatened to kill your wife
And your craven senior officers
Have decided to ruin your life.

Well, stuff them. Stuff the job.
Cut their letters with a razor.
Expose your beating heart
And stop it with a Taser.

61

ANIMAL INSTINCT

You've always worshipped animals
And never loved a human yet.
So you studied hard and won a post
As a rural district vet.

Years passed and you came to learn
A good few things about your
tastes.
You still avoided boyfriend ties
And considered marriage just
a waste.

You treated anything from sheep to
gerbils
But your idyll couldn't last, of course.
Now your reputation lies in tatters
After sexual frolics with a farmer's
horse.

Tonight you take your biggest needle
To smooth away your forehead's
frown.
You plunge it in your waiting thigh
And pentobarbitone soon puts you
down.

BIGGER BROOD

You wanted a bigger family
And fate has borne this out.
But instead of eight sweet
children,
Yours just scream and shout.

They row while at the dinner table
And clamber over chairs.
They've killed your faithful dog
And set fire to the stairs.

Your husband's gone and left -
He couldn't stand the noise.
Your children beat him up
And used his tools as toys.

Tonight when calm returns at last
You find all their baby clothes.
You drench them in a heady
solvent
And tie them to your nose.

63

LADY SCOUT

You relished wearing uniform.
It made you feel so very tall.
It never really registered:
You didn't command respect at all.

Even when you led the scouts,
They considered you an awful
frump.
Bagheera was your chosen name
But this old panther's quite a chump.

Things went well till one sad day
Reality dawned in searing pain.
No-one cared about lady scouts -
Your efforts to shine were just
in vain.

Tonight you make a silent vow
To set sneering neighbours' eyes
a-goggle.
You hang yourself naked from
a tree -
Knot secured by your favourite
woggle.

64

SUPERIOR

You've always been a staunch
believer
In genes of purest white.
Whenever there are brains about
You expect the skin is light.

Paleskins only ruled the world
To save 'browns' and 'blacks' alike.
This has been your personal slogan,
Raised upon a mental pike.

But things are changing at your club
Where you've just been trounced at
chess.
Not only was the victor a woman,
She was also a lawyer Negress.

With members' laughter still ringing
And your mind on her elegant pout,
You sit at home with your shotgun
And blow your superior brains out.

65

HIGH NOTE

For many years after homework
You taught yourself to play guitar.
You never considered university.
In the mirror posed a star.

Bands you played in came and went,
With dead end jobs to make ends
meet.
Decades passed in lowly flats
Whiffing of armpits and sweaty
feet.

Crumpled hopes and broken
strings
Have now finally slowed your pace.
Even your gleaming electric guitar
Lies forlornly in its case.

Tonight you'll plug it in again,
Pound out the chords and laugh.
You'll sip beer, smoke, turn up
the sound,
Then play it in the bath.

DUN ROAMIN'

You've often wanted to travel the world
But have settled on England's
Green Belt.
With your lurchers and snares you
plunder the land.
From a distance your camp can
be smelt.

A traveller's life was the one meant
for you
With its benefits and human rights
laws.
But caravan living is not comfy
enough.
You're starting to see your
lot's flaws.

You'd rather live in a mansion,
Like ones you see down country
lanes.
But at 71 you're too old to break out
And your bones are giving you pains.

Tonight while the camp is deserted,
With a bubbling hare in the pot,
You'll cuddle your best hunting rifle,
Kiss the barrel, and take one last shot.

67

LAST DRINK

You're a lifelong teetotaller
Who'd never touch a drop.
When all around you binge drank
You'd wish that they would stop.

Lager, beer and wine
Would never have you beat.
You'd stick to lemonade
As others took their vodka neat.

But your wife enjoyed a tipple
So your marriage soon broke up.
Your resolve was sorely tested
And you've taken your first sup.

Now the shame is overwhelming.
You can very barely stand.
You jump before a city tram
With a whisky in your hand.

68

BIG ONE

You've fished in lakes and rivers.
You've reeled in salmon and pike.
You've captured perch and carp
And trundled home upon your bike.

You've often had a tale to tell
About the one that got away.
It was always bigger than the rest
Or at least that's what you'd say.

But today you almost did catch
An amazing, real-life beast.
Yet no-one believes a word of it
Until your voice has almost ceased.

Outraged, you get on your bike
again,
And cycle to the deepest lake.
You plunge in with your waders on -
Your end will be no fishy fake.

69

TERMINATED

You're terminally ill.
It's not very nice.
You've lived quite unhealthily.
You're paying the price.

You spend days worrying.
You're awake at night.
The grinning Grim Reaper
Has you in sight.

All the sex you had,
The drugs and the drink
Have taken your life force
And forced you to think.

You buy one last booze crate.
You laugh and then glug,
Snort coke, tell the Reaper:
'Just pull the damn plug !'

CATGUTTED

You thought yourself intelligent
Until you got a cat.
Now you feel a simpleton
With a dunce's hat.

The finest food and drink
Your haughty pet enjoys.
But she disdains your feelings
And with these often toys.

You're always running after her
Because you need a cuddle.
The human/pet relationship
Is rather in a muddle.

And then she runs away
Because she's found a nicer
house.
In your grief you choke yourself
On her plastic mouse.

71

SWINGER

You and hubby liked to swing.
As morals go, it's fine.
Your relationship seemed strong
enough -
And the extra sex divine !

For years you'd like to titillate
Anyone you fancied.
But now hubby's into darker stuff,
His tastes have turned quite
rancid.

You no longer wish to witness
His buttocks being beaten.
Or see his playmates' scat games
With results of what they've eaten.

Tonight when he's set off again
For his weekly sexual ration,
You'll take out a knitting needle
And stab yourself with passion.

72

GLOBAL HARMING

You've always been quite worried
That the ice caps have been
shrinking
And the fate of polar wildlife
Causes disquiet in your thinking.

You hate the way the planet
Is so locked into self-harming.
There seems no way to flee
The effects of global warming.

Now you've gone and tucked
yourself
Into a chilly sealed cellar
And abandoned any furniture
Like some modern cave dweller.

In the darkness you start singing,
(For this task you will not stint)
As you summon carbon monoxide
To reduce your carbon footprint.

73

CUDDLES

You were married for decades
When life seemed just great.
Now your partner is dead
And you're sick of your fate.

No-one to hold you.
No-one to touch.
The lack of a cuddle
Is getting too much.

You've tried dating afresh
But you're simply too old.
You slump in an armchair
Afraid of the cold.

Tonight you take out a picture
Of your dearly departed.
'I'm coming !', you pledge
As the chainsaw gets started.

74

BALD TRUTH

You lost all your hair at 21 -
A fate that shocked your friends.
But you took to wearing wigs
And hoped this made amends.

Your football skills still served
you well,
Playing for your pub's team.
With several glued-on wigs
in place,
The league's top score sheet was
your dream.

But one sad day you rose to head
A ball which shot into the net,
And your wig flew off in
fast pursuit:
A dismal sight that made you fret.

A local paper stuck the picture
Smack bang on its front page.
Tonight you'll dangle from
a crossbar
To bare your sorrow and your rage.

75

STALKER

You started first with informal chats
Aimed at pictures on your walls.
Then you moved to long discussions
With celebrities who never called.

Famous people loathed to spy
Your peering face at their homes'
borders.
So much so they often bugged you
With their tiresome restraining
orders.

Miles and miles you'd trudge
each day
Just to glimpse your favourite star.
But she's hurt your feelings now.
She's called the police and gone
too far.

Tonight you're out on bail again.
You'll spot her good and quick.
You'll set yourself ablaze for love
In what will be your final trick.

76

MEANINGLESS

Life used to have meaning.
It used to have aims.
Now you're sick to the teeth
Of life's silly games.

You built up your business.
You married your bride.
But where is the pay-off?
Where is the pride?

Retirement was meant to be
Something fantastic.
But joy is curtailed
While boredom's elastic.

Tonight on the golf course
You'll howl at the moon,
Drink bleach under stars
And join them quite soon.